Fifty Sheds Darker

R.C. Mood Book 1

Fanny Banghard

Copyright © @50Sheds 2013

Lost Woods

ISBN: 9-781-48408-844-9

The right of @50Sheds to be identified as the author
of this work has been asserted by them in accordance
with the Copyright, Designs and Patents Act 1988.

**Fifty Sheds Darker™ and 50 Sheds Darker™
are trademarks of the author and publisher.**

A CIP catalogue record for this book is available from
the British Library.

For Papa. Who was always firm with me.

CONTENTS

ACKNOWLEDGMENTS

To true love.

1 LEAVING HOME

"Fanny Banghard you will get this job!"

But no matter how confidently I say it to my reflection - I still feel nervous.

You see I've been living in London for just over a month, everyday applying for jobs, trying to catch a break. Out of the blue I receive a phone call from a secretary with a cold voice, her icy personality oozes through the phone. Thankfully she has some heartwarming news. I'm the only American candidate to be selected for an interview with the illustrious Mr. R.C. Mood. He's a self-made billionaire who has a reputation for being abrupt with his staff.

I was beginning to think that all the years I'd spent studying for my degree had been wasted, but I sent in my resumé and my micro-bikini modeling shots and got a call back almost straight away. Mr. Mood is looking for a P.A. to work on an 'unusual assignment.'

I check myself one last time in the mirror. My pencil skirt suit fits like a glove. My caramel brown hair is straight over my shoulders with just the right amount of strands casually draped on my chest to keep me looking professional. My white blouse is perfectly ironed although the top button looks like its set to burst. Oh why can't they make blouses for size zero girls who have a natural pair of 30 DD breasts?

Beep… Beep… Beep... My phone alarm goes off. It's 8 am. DOUBLE CRAP I'm going to be late!

***

2 THE INTERVIEW

One bus and one smelly tube ride later I
sign in with security at the Mood
Industries building. I take the elevator to
the highest story and I walk out onto the
lusciously carpeted floor.

All I see is luxurious glass and chrome. Everything is quiet. I walk over to an office with two huge mahogany doors. The nameplate says *Mr. R.C. Mood.*

I knock. I hear a bit of commotion then a minute later out comes a slender blonde secretary bimbo with a notebook and tussled hair, nervously wiping the corners of her mouth "Sorry to keep you waiting, I was just taking something down!"

She ushers me into the office. There in front of me is the most beautiful example of a man. He is tall and handsome and makes a half-hearted effort at a welcoming smile that doesn't quite reach his eyes.

He shakes my hand and HOLY HELL I feel electricity! I hate it when carpets attract static.

He invites me to sit on the chair in front of his desk then he casually sits on his desk. As an accomplished billionaire I can tell he has a sizeable endowment.

"I'm here to interview you for a very unique job opportunity."

I can tell by his accent that he's played tennis in France.

He starts asking me questions to find out more about me.

"Ms. Banghard that's an exotic name you have, where did you get it from?"

I nervously reply "My parents."

He must be able to see that my mouth is dry he asks, "Would you like a glass of water?"

I shake my head in refusal "Can I have a cup of coffee? I think I'm still a little bit drunk from last night."

R.C. Mood then starts with the formal questioning, "Can you give me three words to describe yourself?"

"Low. Emotional. Quotient. I hardly ever know what the people around me are thinking or feeling. It always gets me into trouble and frustrates everyone else around me!"

"Can you think of a time you made a mistake in a job, and what you did to rectify it?"

"I once took my manager's laptop without asking and forgot to return it, so I had to pay for its replacement."

R.C. Mood shuffles some papers on his desk "I'm a busy man, with a very firm opinion and want my instructions to be carried out immediately and without question. Now, can you tell me why you left your last job?"

I candidly reply, "I have a problem with authority."

Somewhat gruffly R.C. Mood asks, "Why should I hire you?"

"Because I would be a real benefit to your events team as I like to party all the time."

"Okay, we don't seem to be getting anywhere, let's try a different tact."

He stares at my resumé, which I nervously clutch just under my breasts.

"You *look* like the right woman for the job I'd like to see your credentials."

So I show him my best assets.

"I see you have overcome the challenges of dyslexia. So what are your weaknesses?"

"I can't walk past an ice-cream van without stopping for a sixty-nine."

I see the quiver of a smile on his oh-so-handsome face. "Everything appears to be in order."

R.C. Mood seems so formal. He is Mr. Mood, the businessman in the suit. But what do his friends call him? If I were his friend what would he let me call him? Mr R.C. ? Or just R.C. for short? *Arsey!*

"I will keep this brief…

"I've been having some trouble. I am R.C. Mood. I come from the noble family of Mood. The Mood Manor House has been in my family since my great, great, great, great, grandfather returned from the Americas with a ship full of snuff, a rotting pegleg and an itchy crotch to remind him of all the bawdy nights he spent with gummy wenches.

Everything had been tickety-boo until recently. Somebody has been letting our horses out of the stables, secretly milking our cows, mooing at the sheep and punching our chickens.

Overcome with horror I can't help myself exclaim "Oh my God that must be awful for you?"

"It is." He says. "And the chickens are not very happy about it either."

Arsey continues, "Then all our sheds were set on fire. At first we thought the strange attacks were the work of the chav family who moved here from Croydon but then this..."

He proceeds to open a draw in his desk, pulls out a note that he passes to me, it reads:

R.C. Mood, your animals are just the start. You think you can get away with murder but you can't and I want revenge. I won't stop until I have Mood blood on my hands. You will be dead before the Last Moon of June.

When Arsey sees my eyes move up from the letter he says, "That's just over a week away – and before you ask, no I haven't murdered anyone."

"Oh my God! Who on Earth could ever want to hurt you?" I exclaim, perhaps a little too loudly. His eyes soften. For a second I think I see through his armour.

"How can I help," I ask, "I'm not a detective?"

"I know that, that's precisely why I've fingered you for this job."

Arsey explains "This deranged screwball knows the inner workings of Mood Manor so he is obviously in the vicinity of my family home. But the town policeman seems to think it's just an elaborate prank."

"I will hire you as a governess to help around the grounds. I want you to be my eyes and ears and report to me any strange comings and goings. It's important you do this right because my life is in danger."

Who would want to wound this wonderful magical man? Why would they want to torment him?

Arsey waits for me to finish thinking then says "Lastly, do you have any questions for me?"

I pause for a second then come out with a good one, "If you were a fruit, what fruit would you be?"

 "Ms. Banghard. There is something about you. Something I can't quite put my finger on that is… different. Unique. Intriguing." Then like a mad man he shouts "*NO*" to himself. "*This is not a road I will go down again!*" And with that he ushers me out of his office. As the door closes behind me I lean on it, look up to the ceiling and bite my lip.

My heart is beating faster. I feel a tightness in my chest, either this is the start of love or I have heartburn again.

"Oh Arsey, Arsey. Arsey how wonderful it is to say your name with my virgin tongue! What is it that troubles you so? Can I help make you better?"

I'm then startled by the sound of clip-clopping high heel shoes. Secretary Bimbo comes over to me and asks, "Are you okay?"

3 THE ROAD TO CRICKERTY WICKE

Monday morning. It's a long silent journey with Arsey in the front passenger seat talking to his driver. We travel in silence. I notice him using the mirror in the sun visor to look at me repeatedly. It's getting really annoying. What does he think I'm going to do, steal the leather of the seats?

I then start wondering about his initials. R.C. What could the R possibly stand for, most likely something posh? Is he a Raymond? A Reginald? Perhaps a Rudolph?

4 MOOD MANOR

We finally reach the small town of
Crickerty Wicke. We drive past a number
of small, quaint village buildings. We
drive for about 10 minutes more and
approach the grounds of Mood Manor.
Our limo approaches the foreboding
black gates they open and as we drive
through I wonder what it is I have signed
up for. I see a massive mansion; the aged
walls proudly boast that it has a history.
But I suspect it has some secrets too…

Exhausted the butler takes me to my quarters with a four-poster bed. I eat the sandwiches and drink the tea then sleep. I wake up feeling cold. I take a shower and am summoned to the music room by Arsey in a message delivered by the butler. It must be urgent because as I step outside the shower door, wearing nothing but a towel, the butler is waiting to give it to me.

I meekly tread into the warmly lit music parlour with my red dress elegantly clinging to my curves.

Arsey immediately stands to attention "So lovely to see you!" He ejaculates.

The room has a grand piano and is filled with all sorts of different instruments.

It's clear that Arsey is also an accomplished musician – I bet he can handle any instrument.

Arsey wants me to show him my talents.

So I start shaking my maracas in his face.

I ask, "Do you think I've got rhythm?"

Reassuringly he says, "Sure, you look like you can shake it all night long!"

I tell him that I cannot hold a note.

He says, "I bet I can make you sing like a nightingale."

Arsey picks up the saxophone, walks over to me, and starts playing a melancholy tune. His fingering is really good!

When he finishes I feel so relaxed.

He asks me if I want to play with anything so I start tonguing his trombone.

Maybe he's a bit precious about me touching it because he's standing upright.

I take my fingers of the shaft and I can see he's impressed with my blowing technique.

As I leave the room I feel my heart beating faster I realise I'm developing feelings for him. Flustered I go to bed and rock myself to sleep.

5 BROKEN DREAMS

In the haze of my sleep my dreams are troubled. I hear torturous wailing in the distance; I then have the distinct feeling that I am being watched. I wake up shivering; the wind has loosened the window. It's probably just the high ceilings and cold corridors that are giving me nightmares. But it's my first morning in Mood Manor so I'm eager to get started with my assignment. I'm resolved to find the person who would hurt my lovely Arsey.

As I go down to breakfast I bump into Lady Mood. She looks like a wicked headmistress. Her thin shoulders are jutting out of her black dress. Her grey hair is pulled back so tight into a bun that it hides the wrinkles on her forehead. Her skin is jaundiced and sallow. She has a bitter look on her face; she's drinking a gin and lemon juice.

"Welcome Ms. Banghard, we've been expecting you." But her kind words are at odds with her frosty voice. I return the pleasantries. She looks me up and down and I can see her eyes judging me.

"My-my you have a sweet apple pie smile – it's enough to tempt a lesser man."

It sounds like a compliment but it doesn't feel like one.

"My mom always told me that smiling sweetly made me sweeter."

Lady Mood's eyebrows raise an inch, "The problem with sweet things is that they appear nice but ultimately they are bad for you. They make you fat!"

I get the message! She may look frail but when it comes to Arsey she will protect him as ferociously as a lioness does her cubs. She doesn't think I'm good enough. She is warning me off.

"Thankfully my Richard's tastes are more refined."

"HE'S A DICK!"

"Excuse me?"

"Oh, I don't mean anything unkind. I didn't realise your son is a Dick."

Lady Mood seems somewhat taken aback by this. "Regardless, we are appreciative of your efforts to help our family. My eyesight gets worse every year but I can see well enough to know you are sincere. Not every Lady in an expensive dress is…"

She then bids me farewell and leaves the Manor to get into her waiting Rolls Royce.

6 HAMISH MCGRIND

After breakfast the butler takes me to the servants quarters and introduces me to the Groundskeeper Hamish McGrind. He has a wiry beard, a glint in his eye and a self-levitating kilt. I politely greet him "Good Morning sir."

"You're a bonny lass with a tempting figure – I don't imagine it was your resumé that made Mr. Mood hire you."

I don't know what he means exactly but it doesn't sound respectful "Well actually I have a lot of experience." I retort.

"I bet you have! There's nothing I like more than a girl with experience."

McGrind then asks me "How's your Father?!"

I reply "Fine, thank you for asking," but the puzzled look on his face suggests that wasn't the answer he was hoping for.

He looks wistfully at a portrait of a fierce looking woman with freckles, ginger hair and a shadow on her top lip. "My wife is currently in prison. She's doing ten years for an assault on a cigar-smoking circus monkey.

Before she went down she would always make me laugh."

McGrind says, "I should count my blessings. I work in the beautiful outdoors, I have a kindly boss, I've been doing this job for years and I've no problems with any of my equipment."

Outside. I open the cage door to the aviary and a blue tit hops out on to my hand, and then another. McGrind walks past, peers over my arm and almost beside himself says, "That's a lovely pair of tits you've got there."

They fly into a nearby tree. I try and recall a *proverb* my dad taught me "Two in the bush is better than one in the hand." He seems flummoxed.

McGrind wanders of into the gardens,
after ten minutes of searching I find him
near the animal cages. He has a big cock
in his hands. Somebody had left the
chicken coup open.

Almost beating his chest with self-pride McGrind boasts, "You know I've seen plenty of action."

Wanting to know more I ask "Were you in the war?"

"No."

McGrind has terrible arthritis but continues to work in the cold. He laments, "I'm getting a bit stiff, would you like to stop for a bit?"

I agree to go with him to hunt pheasants. He leads me far away from the Manor House. When we get to the woods he says, "I'm game if you are!" So I shoot him.

Thankfully the bullet just scrapes his cheek, but he's not impressed. I run off deeper into the woods to escape his fury.

Exhausted. I collapse and slump back on to the root of a large tree, and loosen the buttons of my skirt. A couple of ants start crawling up my naked thigh.

I busily start flicking away then McGrind walks by, when I see the look on his face I think he is going to finish me off!

7 FISHING

The next morning Arsey meets me after breakfast and requests that we go fishing and have a picnic in the forest. We walk for 30 minutes until we reach Lagoon Lake and he prepares his tackle.

As he is sitting and playing with his equipment I think it is a good time to get to know him by asking him a few questions. "Tell me about the first time you went fishing?"

"I went for a holiday to Bournemouth. I had planned to go fishing but got distracted. I caught crabs at the seaside."

Gingerly I ask, "Have you ever been in love?" But I think I already know the answer.

"I fell in love with Italy; the food, the scenery, the women. For about a year I was in and out of Florence."

"Then I met Countess Emilia Peroni of Monaco, a fine-looking woman who is both graceful and determined. We were to be married in a lavish ceremony on a Croatian mountaintop overlooking a glittering blue sea. But it wasn't to be..."

A sad look tugs on his face. I cannot tell if it is relief or regret.

I see no point in pushing for further information. With my questioning over Arsey's demeanor suddenly changes for the better and with a cheeky grin he boasts, "I'm going to show you every trick I know.'

He flicks the line into the water.

I see him struggling. He yells "Quick, grab hold of my rod!"

I run over and wrap both my hands around it and we tug it together.

I see something come flying towards me then feel a thud on my head.

It's over a foot long! Arsey has a self-satisfied look on his face.

"It's a whopper!"

8 BARN ROMANCE

It starts to rain, hard heavy rain. Then turns to hailstones. OW!

Arsey picks up a bag and shouts, "It's too dangerous to stay under the sky, and we are too far from home."

He grabs my hand. "Quick there's a barn nearby, which I built myself. But it needs more work done to stabilise it."

We run, I almost trip but he has me. Oh but how I wish he had me!

We bolt into a huge barn that looks beautiful if a little unsteady. On seeing its full height I proclaim "What an enormous erection!" But it seems a little precarious. Arsey says, "I hope it will hold up."

"So do I!"

He takes off his shirt and reveals a beautiful body that looks chiseled by the hands of the ancient gods. I can't help but compliment him "You look like you can handle yourself!"

He explains, "growing up without any friends you could say I had to."

Like a spoilt child I complain, "I'm gushing wet."

Arsey grins, "It's time to heat things up a bit."

"That's a great idea, can you build a campfire?"

He petulantly finds some logs and passes them to me as I set them up in a circle I ask, "Are there enough to keep the fire burning?"

With a smirk he says, "I've got more wood than you can handle."

As the fire flickers warmly we start to talk. Arsey is strangely quiet so I try to make conversation.

Arsey tells me that he recently returned from a business trip to Australia. I see he is playing around with something in his left trouser pocket. "What have you got there?" I ask him.

"Just something I picked up Down Under."

Arsey pulls out a bag of marbles, some are white with black streaks, some are multi-coloured. I notice that when he plays with his balls it brings a joyous glee to his face.

He stares at me intensely then asks, "For an American city-high flyer you don't seem to be afraid of the animals, why is that?"

I reply warmly "As a girl I used to groom the horses on the local farm. I would feed them, clean them, brush them and train them to gallop across any type of terrain without injuring them. As such I can confidently say I am the best ride in town."

His face changes, he is hurting, I want to soothe away his fear. He is fighting with himself to open up and then he does. "I know I can be a bit stiff but all I want is to meet someone who I can be myself with. You seem like you can get to grips with my hardness and help soften me up."

He looks at me longingly and says, "I'd like to slip into something more comfortable."

I open my bag and pass him my pink M&S cardigan.

Arsey looks at my mouth, his eyes imploring me "You don't understand, I want you to make me feel like a man!"

"Okay" I say " Give me £500 to go shopping then you can piss off down the pub."

When the heavy rains finally stop we head back to Mood Manor. We get back and I'm concerned that his mother, the strict Lady Mood, will scold me for coming in late. Arsey offers to take me up the back passage, and I accept. *"Oh my Arsey, why do you hurt so much?"* I can't stop thinking about this poor tormented mercurial man.

9 A NEW DAWN

The next morning I receive a phone call from my mom, my papa is worried about me so my mom is repeating to him everything I say. I tell her about Arsey kindly offering to take me fishing. She translates it to "The gentleman offered to show our Fanny a good time."

I tell her how I helped Arsey with his fishing rod and it started raining.

I hear her say, "He let her hold his pole and she got wet."

Mom tells me how it's raining hard back in Kansas and I tell how it rained so heavy here in England that we had four inches of rain. My mom says to my papa "Would you believe it? Fanny's had *four* inches!"

I go for a walk to visit the tits and the cocks. When I get back to Mood Manor there is a young woman in cream jockey shorts waiting at the stables. She's got shiny platinum hair that perfectly catches the sun. She confidently strides over to me with her hands on her wiggling hips. She introduces herself "Hello there Fanny, I've been hoping to bump into you!"

I hear an Irish twang in her voice. I can tell from her accent that she's a vegetarian.

"I am Ms. Bien. Leslie Bien, but all the women at the Auxiliary club call me Lez.

There is something very queer about her, I think it's the shamrock necklace she's wearing.

We get talking and she's friendly enough. She works as Lady Mood's chief stable hand. Like me, she's also away from home. She's from Muff, Donegal, Ireland.

I tell her I'm a trophy winning Kansas jockey.

She says, "That's great! Too many people forget their roots but I will never forget the hobby clubs that gave me opportunities. I am a gold medal winning Muff swimmer, a fast Muff cycler and a proud Muff diver."

Lez asks me if I want to trim her mound but I don't know how to use a garden strimmer.

10 CHINESE TAKE AWAY

Arsey is away on business and I don't want to eat in the dining hall alone. So I catch a lift into town and head to the local Chinese take-away Kok & Kin.

Mr. Kin runs it. Arsey has been going there for years so the food is highly recommended. But I need to get to know Mr. Kin in my search for clues. I ask him what his first name is, he says "Wan." Wan Kin is the sort of person who is always cheerful for one reason or another.

He certainly seems friendly enough. I can tell because he is eyeing me up and down and smiling. He then asks me something but I feel like *'the Rude American'* because I'm having difficulty understanding his accent. He repeats his question "Would you like a fork?" But I haven't even ordered yet.

I say, "I'm in the mood to taste something a little bit different."

Wan says "how about a nice bit of fish?"

"I've tried it once but much as I've thought about it fish isn't for me."

Wan makes another suggestion "How about you get your mouth around my delicious spicy balls?"

I think "Why not!" When he puts them in front of me I gobble them up quick-time. I can see he is happy I tucked in!

Just as I'm leaving Wan's brother walks in. "Hi," I say "I'm Banghard, Fanny Banghard."

He smiles kindly "Kok. Chew Kok."

11 DENTIST

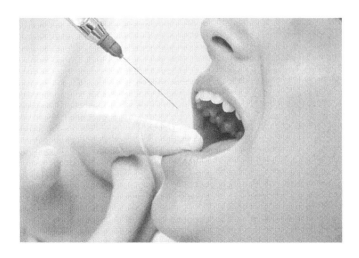

During breakfast I bite too hard on a rock cake and feel a sharp pain in my tooth.

Hamish McGrind rushes me to the dentist in the back of his luminous green Ford Capri.

I go in and accept the dentist's invitation to sit. Can a person be over friendly?

He immediately knows the precise spot to put his finger – "OW!" I'm feeling very tender.

I meekly say to him "I'm worried that it will hurt"

He grins "I can help you with that. Don't be afraid you will just feel a little prick."

After a couple of minutes he brings his instrument near me and asks me to "open wide." The whole experience isn't as daunting as I thought it would be, five minutes later and he's getting me to rinse and spit.

12 THE RAM'S BOTTOM

Arsey returns from London and asks me if I want him to put something nice in my mouth.

I say, "I'd love you to! I saw a nice English pub in town that sells hot dinners."

We walk in to the Ram's Bottom and they're hosting a USA theme night! They have a bucking bronco ride and Arsey dares me to get on. I can't help but feel a sense of nervous anticipation I bite my lip and ask him "Will it jerk me off?"

We bump into an old friend of Arsey's from boarding school. A part-time Territorial Army captain named Lafayette LeBatti. He's here with his men.

Arsey says, "He was my fag at Eaton Hall Boarding School."

"He was a very queer fellow. He was always hanging around the rear entrance."

"He joined the army and it changed him. When he came back he was always singing camp songs."

We walk over to LeBatti and he seems absolutely delighted to see my Arsey, who after a minute of their bear hug introduces me to LeBatti.

He's a lively fellow. When I ask him what he does for a day job he tells me he's an events manager and he enjoys holding policemen's balls.

Arsey tells me they used to both act in school plays. "He had a bigger part than me, how times change I now have a bigger part than him."

Arsey leads us over to the bar to buy us all a drink. LeBatti says he wants a rum and Coke, Arsey orders a small vodka and orange which is one of my favourite drinks so I ask for 'a large one.'

After a few rounds I'm left alone and bored, as everyone seems to be talking to everybody else.

It's been a really stressful day and I eye the barman who's holding a bottle of vodka. He asks me what I want and I say, "I could really do with a stiff one."

I think he must have thought I'd been drinking all night because he replies "It looks like you've had a few already."

LeBatti pulls out his camera and starts taking pictures of anyone who'll let him. Arsey pulls him over and commands 'I want you to take a picture of me and my beautiful Fanny.'

He said *my* Fanny! I can feel my heartbeat doing the Merengue.

Half an hour later a fight breaks out between a gang of lads and three of LeBatti's off-duty soldiers. After a couple of minutes a policeman comes storming in. He pulls out his truncheon and starts waving it around without a thought or a care for who he whacks with it.

He then scolds LeBatti for the bad behavior of his soldiers. "I suggest you check on your privates."

I'm feeling lonely because Arsey has been neglecting me and I've now had a few too many. The policeman walks past me as I drunkenly lean on the bar. With a coquettishly drunk smile on my face I ask him "Are you going to read me my rights?"

But he doesn't.

I'd gone into the Ram's Bottom to eat and drink with Arsey with nothing but a smile, a sexy walk and my tightly fitted v-neck dress, by the end of the night I was falling out.

13 VICAR

The following morning I wake up with a heavy head and a heavier heart. Why does my darling mercurial Arsey blow hot and cold on me?

After breakfast the butler says there is someone to see me, it's the parish vicar. The butler leads him in and politely gives him a formal introduction.

"This is Father Tobias who has been with our community for over 26 years. Did you know our Vicar likes to play on his organ?

"The Vicar is also a composer. I particularly admire his movements." The butler then turns around and leaves.

He kindly greets me, "Good morning dear you must be the glamorous Ms. Banghard. Lady Mood has told me of your stay here."

He must really want to talk to someone because he starts telling me his problems. Apparently the Bishop visited the vicar for a week but was forever criticising him. The vicar confides in me that he wanted to let off steam in an unorthodox manner "I know I am a man of the cloth but sometimes I really did feel like flogging the bishop."

Anyway, he is raising funds to repair the church roof and asks me if I can help him on the antiques and bakery stalls at the summer fete on Saturday. I think it is a great opportunity to meet all the faces from the town so I agree.

The vicar must have heard that I'm good at cake making because he offers to help me put a bun in the oven.

Fanny Banghard

14 SUMMER FETE

Saturday morning. The sun is shining.
And the car park is filled with helpers
hawking their wares to the community.

The vicar gives me some advice. "Keep an eye out for young oiks who sneak up on you when you are not looking as they're always touching things." Thankfully I'm transferred from the bric-à-brac to the furniture stall.

I want to make myself useful and actually make sales so when a young father comes along holding his daughter's hand. I try my best sales pitch "Can I interest you in a nice little dresser without any draws?"

His eyes almost pop out of his head. Maybe Crickerty Wicke is suffering from a shortage of good quality carpentry?

He just stares at me so I draw his attention to something else "Sir would you care to take a look, I have a beautiful chest that I know you'll love."

Later I help out on the bakery stall. A crowd of hungry builders gathers around, drawn in by the delicious smells of hot pastries. I can be very clumsy, so I try extra hard not to drop anything down my cleavage again as my yellow polka dot summer dress is low cut at the front and shows up my tardiness.

When the builders see my muffins they all crowd around me with a ravenous look on their faces - they won't go away until I beat them off!

After a hard days work the Vicar thanks
me for my help and gives me a lift back
to my temporary home, Mood Manor.

15 MY ARSEY

The next morning before breakfast I have a swim in the indoor pool to try and settle myself. After I come out I rub myself dry.

I overhear McGrind say to the butler that Arsey returned last night. I can't contain myself any longer and feel myself exploding.

I storm into his bedroom expecting him to be sleeping like a baby but he is sitting on his bed with the covers fallen to one side "Morning Arsey, you're up early!'

Back from his trip to Liverpool he is playing around with something just under his waist. "What have you got there?" I ask him.

Blushing he says "My marbles. I was just knocking them together."

In my rush to speak to him my towel has fallen to my waist exposing my sheer cream bikini top. "I hope this isn't inappropriate but there is something I want to get off my chest." Arsey says, "Now is as good a time as any…" He pauses then says with a Cheshire grin "… I see you can be a real handful"

But I'm not in the mood for humour. Trying to hold back the tears that are queuing at the back of my eyes I say, "I came here to help you but I don't understand you. You are always blowing hot and cold on me. If you don't want me here then tell me to go."

"Fanny, my dear fanny." He beckons me over with his hand. I look down ignoring his plea.

"Fanny, don't be stubborn. All I want you to do is come"

I walk over to him.

"I used to think that I don't deserve to be happy.

"You don't realise how much you've changed me. I was a block of glacier ice, but you've thawed my heart. Now I'm just a damp spot."

He pushes my hair behind my ear then half-whispers "I want to hear you moan for me!"

I reply, "Well you can be inconsiderate, and you've never sent me flowers."

"I want to get you in the right mood. How about we watch something dirty?"

"Alright" I say. "How about we stare at your windows, it looks like they haven't been cleaned for years."

Arsey strokes my neck and soothingly says, "I want to know you biblically."

So I offer to take him with me to my Sunday Studies class.

"Fanny, I want to do something I've never done before"

"What, eat with your mouth closed?"

I slip out of his beautifully warm hands and walk over to the window. He gets out of bed wearing nothing but a thong. He is majestic, but he is oblivious to the feelings I have inside.

He walks over to me, grabs my shoulders. I feel electricity shoot through my body. Why does he have so much static carpet? He seems mad with rage like he is about to hit me; by I am so hungry for his touch that I would gladly accept whatever I can get.

He looks into my eyes, and says. Fanny, dear Fanny and he kisses me! A BEAUTIFUL MEANINGFUL KISS! Thank god he is holding me because I think I might faint.

My heart is pounding, he is looking at me and I'm looking at him. He is so strong yet so tender with me. *This* is something. This is a moment I want to never end. We are both staring into each other's eyes and for a moment it feels like we could stay like this forever.

BAM. His bedroom door bursts open. It is his chauffeur. "Sir, there is an urgent matter. Countess Emilia is visiting from Monaco and requires your immediate attention in London. Arsey leaps into his trousers, throws on a shirt, grabs his jacket, turns back to glance once into my eyes and then is gone. Leaving me alone to survey the bombsite of my heart.

***

16 MISSING

Arsey finally opens up to me then disappears on urgent business, with *her*. It's been four days and no one has seen or heard from him. I've been left in no-man's land and I don't know what to do. Since he left I have not been able to get out of bed. The butler has come to check on me regularly but it hasn't made a difference.

Even the lovely Lez came to visit me. When I saw her kind eyes I started sobbing. She attempted to lift my spirits. She said, "Look at me, I've had my fair share of knockers, but I don't let any man keep me down."

Lez then tried every trick in her book to arouse me from my depression and go out with her.

She even begged me to go with her to take a turn around the gardens. "Come" she implored. In an attempt to persuade me she soothingly massaged the back of my shoulders but no matter how hard she rubbed me I wouldn't come.

Later, Lady Mood strides into my room "I bring tidings. I have sent for your father and he will arrive tomorrow in time for my grand Sunday dinner."

In an unusual moment of sensitivity she sits on the edge of the bed and kindly smiles at me. "What is it dear? Why are you so forlorn? What has my Dick done to you?"

"Your son. Dick." I say to Lady Mood. "He's not the man I thought he was, the man I hoped he could be."

She says "don't judge him on his shortcomings."

"Men can be terrible. Why is that if you give them an inch of space they want a few more?" I ask rhetorically. At first Lady Mood doesn't seem sure on what to say next then her eyes flash open as she recounts something of her history.

"Before I married my Dick's father, Lord Mood, I was engaged to a man who always wanted more. But he got so cocky that I broke it off."

"Now stop your bellyaching, brush your hair and go and help cook with the preparations for tomorrow. When we welcome your father I want him to see you at your best."

17 PREPARATION

Cook is a big tubby man with tubby fingers and thumbs. His face is pink, shiny and bloated. But he's friendly and more than happy to show me around his kitchen.

"On the menu today is beef and Yorkshire pudding with cockerel for those who like a bit of game!"

He explains where he learnt his culinary art; "My dear mother taught me how to cook. Whenever I go home mother makes the most delicious buns. I enjoy icing mother's buns."

"But what I really enjoy is putting my hard dough in a hot oven."

Forward and back, forward and back - cook has the most incredible technique!

I just hope that when it's my turn to roll the pastry it comes out as well.

Cook is making a cake and asks me "I've got something sweet for you, do you want to try some?"

I reply "Not now, but I might later. Whenever it gets to bedtime I'm always trying to shove something in my mouth."

Cooks hairy pink belly hangs over his apron. I ask him how he got so big and he explains, "I make French fries to keep my energy levels up when I'm cooking. Do you fancy a portion?"

Cook is going to tenderise the beef. He wants me to help him with the salad. He pulls out the most ginormous cucumber!

I go to the largest fridge to take out the cockerel. When I turn around I see Cook behind the food counter looking down, furiously moving his right arm. He's beating the meat.

I hear a lot of commotion outside the window. But a tree is blocking the view. A car has arrived – it's papa! I hear Lady Mood welcome him and report on my melancholy. He obviously cares about what makes me happy as I hear him say to Lady Mood "My Fanny and your Dick should be together."

"Yes." says lady Mood "They make a handsome couple."

Like an impatient schoolgirl happy that her father has come home from work I run out and hug him tighter than I ever have before.

18 DINNER

Sunday afternoon and I'm sitting at the dining table with the most unusual mix of people; Lady Mood, Hamish McGrind, LeBatti, papa and me. Lez Bien is expected but she is running late, her empty seat is waiting for her.

Lady Mood asks me how it went in the kitchen. "I was busy preparing the cock so we could all eat it. Cook helped me with my stuffing.

McGrind is carving up the pheasant, talking about a good bit of leg and thighs and rump.

"What piece is your favourite Ms. Fanny?"

"I used to like a nice bit of leg but Lez Bien has been instrumental in getting me to taste something new, so right now I'm partial to a bit of breast."

Lady Mood knows how to entertain her subjects and is a charming raconteur.

"We're all used to the larger animals from working on the farms. What about you Fanny, have you had any pets?"

I reply, " Well, I've had a pussy, a bitch and a cockatoo!"

"Aha! "She cacaws. This morsel of information is enough to energise her "So where do you stand on the cat versus dog debate?"

"Dogs can be ferocious, even puppies. They show their teeth and turn on their owners. But a little pussy never hurt anyone."

Just at that moment Lez strides into the room and proudly shouts "Here! Here!"

LeBatti quiet up until now replies to Lady Mood's question from 5 minutes ago "I've had twelve finches."

Lady Mood's face suddenly turns very stern "Lebatti. Now is not the time to discuss your proclivities."

McGrind offers Lez some pheasant but she churlishly refuses "I don't eat meat."

I lean over the table to offer Lez something from the fruit bowl. Silly me. I stretch a little too far and almost pop out of my French maid style blouse.

I ask her "Do you fancy an apple?"

"Well" she says, "I'd prefer a nice juicy pear."

She must be starving as she has a ravished look on her face.

My papa tries to change the subject. Having heard all about Arsey from Mom he starts making small talk about the English weather.

I can't conceal my loneliness anymore; I say to Lady Mood "I can't wait until your Dick gets in."

The vicar stands up suddenly with an intense look on his face "This involves everyone. I think we should all get things out in the open. I want a mass debate."

"Not now vicar" says Lady Mood, quickly admonishing him with a verbal slap that's force is so strong he collapses back into his seat.

BAM. The dining room doors smash open. "It's my Arsey!"

His clothes are torn. His face is muddy, his lip is cut but he's alive! I pounce on him and give him the biggest hug I can.

Lady Mood smiles – I thought she didn't care but there is so much relief on her face. "My Dick has come home!" She shouts with parental relief.

Arsey explains, "Last week I had to leave suddenly because I received news from my ex-fiancée Countess Emilia Peroni of Monaco that she had acquired intelligence about who is behind the attacks on Mood Manor but had to share it with me in person. I drove to my light aircraft hanger on the north side of Mood grounds. I went in and took out my chopper."

I interject "But there was a thunderstorm that day"

He replies, "I've been told I can handle my chopper like the best of them."

"But as I was flying this idiot was coming up behind me and I had an accident. I crashed, but luckily everything was still in one piece. So I started bashing away at my chopper to get it moving again."

Staring deeply into my eyes he says, "I thought I lost you but one thing kept going over and over in my head."

"What was that?"

"I cannot survive without my Fanny!" I swoon and Arsey catches me.

"There is nothing more I could wish for than to be able to take you up the aisle."

Arsey gets down on his left knee and takes my right hand.

"Fanny. My dear Fanny. Will you do me the honour of making me the happiest man in the world and marrying me."

I explode into tears. Crying. "Yes Yes YES!"

"Darling, there's nothing I want more than to give you a happy ending!"

And everybody in the room spontaneously starts cheering and clapping.

***

"Little Dickie getting married? This will never do…"

Fifty Sheds Darker will be continued in:

R.C. Mood Book 2

You can join in the conversation or contact the author at:

Facebook.com/FiftyShedsDarker

Twitter.com/50Sheds

Photo Acknowledgements

These photos have been used under license from Dreamstime.com:

Saxophone player © Tatiana Morozova

Colorful maracas © Clovercity

Dentist © Diego Vito Cervo

Two Blue Tit Birds feeding on seeds © Rowfam

Funny portrait of hen © Khorzhevska

Roasted Turkey © Ella1977

Pint of Beer © Stuart Monk

Old Shed © Jason Salmon

Hand Point © Orhan Aydeniz

Rain © Bogdanova

Pear © Opel77

Human looking kangaroo © Smileus

Ice cream cone with chocolate flake © Paul Michael Hughes

Cute cream Persian kitten in hammock © Linncurrie

Bombay Accent Chest of Drawers © James Phelps Jr

Fifty Sheds Darker

Wood © Rafał Rynkiewicz

Circus chimpanzee monkey in a suit and a hat. © Innervisionart

Holding carp © Gong Xin

Orange muffins © Tamara Kulikova

Man's and woman's hands on the table © Roman Podvysotskiy

Meat tenderising © Nilsz

Argentine Asado © Noamfein

Flapping coloured flags © Anthony Brown

Sweet and sour pork balls © Stocksolutions

Horsewoman in uniform © Aprescindere

Straw house © Berna Namoglu

Historic English Stately Home © Debu55y

Dramatic Skyscraper © Victor Pelaez Torres

Ram © Anna Mutwil

Trombonist silhouette © Abbitt

Printed in Great Britain
by Amazon.co.uk, Ltd.,
Marston Gate.